WITHDRAWN

WITHDRAWN

silent w
as in wreath

Carey Molter

Consulting Editor Monica Marx, M.A./Reading Specialist

jj 1-2 M

Published by SandCastle™, an imprint of ABDO Publishing Company, 4940 Viking Drive, Edina, Minnesota 55435.

Printed in the United States.

Credits
Edited by: Pam Price
Curriculum Coordinator: Nancy Tuminelly
Cover and Interior Design and Production: Mighty Media
Photo Credits: Eyewire Images, Hemera, ImageState, PhotoDisc, Stockbyte

Library of Congress Cataloging-in-Publication Data

Molter, Carey, 1973-
     Silent W as in wreath / Carey Molter.
         p. cm. -- (Silent letters)
     Includes index.
     Summary: Easy-to-read sentences introduce words that contain a silent "W," such as wreath, two, and answer.
     ISBN 1-59197-448-8
     1. English language--Consonants--Juvenile literature. [1. English language--Consonants.] I. Title.

PE1159.M659 2003
428.1--dc21

2003048129

SandCastle™ books are created by a professional team of educators, reading specialists, and content developers around five essential components that include phonemic awareness, phonics, vocabulary, text comprehension, and fluency. All books are written, reviewed, and leveled for guided reading, early intervention reading, and Accelerated Reader® programs and designed for use in shared, guided, and independent reading and writing activities to support a balanced approach to literacy instruction.

Let Us Know

After reading the book, SandCastle would like you to tell us your stories about reading. What is your favorite page? Was there something hard that you needed help with? Share the ups and downs of learning to read. We want to hear from you! To get posted on the ABDO Publishing Company Web site, send us e-mail at:

sandcastle@abdopub.com

SandCastle Level: Beginning

Silent-w Words

answer

two

wrap

wreath

wrestle

write

The wreath
is green.

Amy likes to wrap presents.

Malik likes
to write letters
to his pen pal.

There are two red boots.

The answer to
two plus two is
four.

The Grant family likes to wrestle together.

The Wren
and Her Kitten

The wren lived in a wreath.
The kitten lived underneath.

The wren had a list
that she wrote.

She put what she wrote in a tote.

The list she had written
was stuff not to buy
for her kitten.

The wren wrote it
so she would not forget

and buy something wrong
for her pet!

More Silent-w Words

sword

who

whole

whom

whose

wrangle

wreck

wring

wrinkle

Glossary

tote   a large bag used to carry things

wrap   to cover a present with paper

wreath   leaves and branches that are twisted together into the shape of a circle

wren   a small, brown songbird with a tail that sticks up

wrestle   to fight or play by grabbing someone and trying to hold him on the ground

About SandCastle™

A professional team of educators, reading specialists, and content developers created the SandCastle™ series to support young readers as they develop reading skills and strategies and increase their general knowledge. The SandCastle™ series has four levels that correspond to early literacy development in young children. The levels are provided to help teachers and parents select the appropriate books for young readers.

Emerging Readers
(no flags)

Beginning Readers
(1 flag)

Transitional Readers
(2 flags)

Fluent Readers
(3 flags)

These levels are meant only as a guide. All levels are subject to change.

ABDO
Publishing Company

To see a complete list of SandCastle™ books and other nonfiction titles from ABDO Publishing Company, visit **www.abdopub.com** or contact us at:

4940 Viking Drive, Edina, Minnesota 55435 • 1-800-800-1312 • fax: 1-952-831-1632